How do some people walk barefoot on red-hot coals? How do others find underground water using only a simple forked stick? (Dowsing has been closely studied by the French Academy of Sciences. They concluded, "It is impossible to deny its existence, although its nature cannot be determined.")

And what about the "flexible" goldfish? Other animals have a fixed growth pattern: they reach a certain size and grow no more. Not so the goldfish. A pet goldfish kept in a small bowl will remain small all its life. Yet the same fish, if kept in a large outdoor pool, may grow to a length of a foot or more.

We may take the size of a goldfish for granted, but it is still a mystery to science. In this lively, thought-provoking text, David Knight presents some amazing and mysterious phenomena. These things "can't" happen—but they do.

Bees Can't Fly,
But They Do

DAVID C. KNIGHT is the author of many popular science books for children, including his recent *Harnessing the Sun: The Story of Solar Energy, Eavesdropping on Space: The Quest of Radio Astronomy, Let's Find Out About Sound, Let's Find Out About Earth,* and his well-known *American Astronauts and Spacecraft.*

BARBARA WOLFF is the illustrator of several science books for children, as well as *December Decorations,* a holiday how-to book by Peggy Parish. She is also the author-illustrator of *Evening Gray, Morning Red,* a book of American weather lore for beginning readers.

Bees Can't Fly,

But They Do

THINGS THAT ARE STILL A MYSTERY TO SCIENCE

BY DAVID C. KNIGHT

Illustrated by Barbara Wolff

J
001.93
Kni

Macmillan Publishing Co., Inc.
NEW YORK
Collier Macmillan Publishers
LONDON

Copyright © 1976 David C. Knight
Copyright © 1976 Macmillan Publishing Co., Inc.
All rights reserved. No part of this book may be reproduced or transmitted in any form or by any means, electronic or mechanical, including photo-copying, recording or by any information storage and retrieval system, without permission in writing from the Publisher.
Macmillan Publishing Co., Inc.
866 Third Avenue, New York, N.Y. 10022
Collier Macmillan Canada, Ltd.
Printed in the United States of America
10 9 8 7 6 5 4 3 2 1

LIBRARY OF CONGRESS CATALOGING IN PUBLICATION DATA
Knight, David C   Bees can't fly, but they do.
SUMMARY: Discusses six phenomena inexplicable to scientists, including the ability of certain people to walk on fire without being burned, the Australian Aborigines' possession of ESP, and the fact that divining rods really work.
1. Natural history—Miscellanea—Juvenile literature.   [1. Natural history—Miscellanea.   2. Curiosities and wonders]   I. Wolff, Barbara.   II. Title.
QH48.K68   001.9'3   76-8491   ISBN 0-02-750860-9

Contents

Bees Can't Fly,
But They Do

Introduction

This book is about some things that seem to defy the laws of nature: people who can find underground water with a simple forked stick, or those who can walk on red-hot coals without being burned. These things "can't" happen—but they do. *How* they happen is still a mystery, even to scientists.

Until fairly recently, it was a mystery how certain large bees, bumblebees in particular, were able to fly.

To aerodynamicists—scientists who study the physical laws of flight—a bee's body seemed too heavy and its wings too small for it to become airborne and remain so. Bees "can't" fly . . . but do. The mystery became so intriguing that a few scientists decided to study it.

Most insects fly by using muscles that flap their wings with great speed. For example, the locust beats its wings at a rate of about 20 times per second to fly. Other flying insects have to beat their wings even faster —perhaps as rapidly as 100 times per second.

But bees must work extra hard to become airborne.

Honeybees, for instance, must beat their wings about 200 times a second to fly. Yet larger bees—like bumblebees—whose bodies are heavier, wider, and longer—have to do even better. The scientists found that to stay aloft, such bees must beat their wings at the amazing rate of 300 times a second or more—a rate that previously was believed impossible. To put it another way, this type of bee has to flap its wings an astonishing 18,000 times to fly for one minute.

Other mysteries haven't been solved yet. For example, there is the enigma of the "flexible" goldfish. Other animals stay within a fixed growth pattern; they reach a certain size and grow no more. So do people and most plants. Not so the goldfish. A pet goldfish kept in a small bowl will remain small all its life. Yet the same fish, if kept in an outdoor pool, may grow to a length of a foot or more.

Occasionally pet goldfish escape from ornamental pools or brooks in parks and gardens into nearby rivers or lakes. They are so adaptable that they do not die but become wild goldfish. They also start to grow again. Some of these wild goldfish that have been caught measure close to two feet. Scientists are puzzled by this flexibility. No other fish adapts itself quite so remarkably to its environment. It's still a mystery.

Likewise, there is the mystery of why trees don't stop growing—still unsolved. Human beings usually stop growing sometime during their teens. Many animals reach full growth within a year. Others are fully grown in just a few years. Birds and insects also stop growing at a certain age. But trees keep growing as long as they live.

Trees live, grow, and reproduce themselves by an amazing process. The thousands of leaves put forth by the tree breathe for it and manufacture all its food. Its root system gathers minerals and vast quantities of water. To carry this water to the leaves, the tree is equipped with an intricate circulation system that extends upward from the millions of root hairs through the trunk and branches. The trunk holds the leaves up to the sunlight, sends them water from the roots, and gets food back from them. Then seeds are borne in flowers or cones.

Year after year, the cycle repeats itself, and the tree grows larger and larger. Only the death of the tree— through human efforts, disease, or some other cause— halts the growing process. For some hardy trees, like the giant Sequoias, that day may still be thousands of years away. Meanwhile, the process of continuous growth goes on. Scientists still cannot explain why trees do not stop growing.

As with the bumblebee, someday someone will find the answer to these mysteries. Few things remain a secret forever. But for now, they are still a mystery.

The Fearless Fire Walkers

Possibly no religious ceremony is as strange—or as potentially dangerous—as walking through fire. The practice of fire walking is centuries old and was known in ancient Greece, India, and China. It still survives today in such widely separated parts of the world as Japan, Malaya, Fiji, Tahiti, and even in Western countries such as Bulgaria and Spain.

Fire walking can be performed in many ways. Usually the barefoot person walks swiftly over a layer of embers or coals spread along the bottom of a narrow trench. Sometimes the person must walk through

14

a blazing log fire or its smouldering ashes. Amazingly, few fire walkers are ever burned.

There are other variations on this art. Instead of embers from a wood fire, the fire walker may have to cross over red-hot stones. Occasionally the embers may be poured over his head in a "fire bath." Or the man may be ordered to lash himself with a flaming torch.

Why should people go through such terrible ordeals by fire? What drives them to it? There seem to be several widespread reasons for this practice. In some societies, if a man—usually a chief or leader—comes through the fire unhurt, he assures his people of a good harvest that year. In other cultures, a man will undertake fire walking to fulfill a vow, such as testing his devotion to his gods or ensuring success in battle against his enemies.

Walking across fire also has been used to prove or disprove a person's innocence. For example, someone accused of committing a crime may be asked to run barefoot through fire. If he comes through with no trace of a burn, he is judged to be not guilty of the crime.

Fire walking and a person's faith in religion seem to go together as well. Fire walkers firmly believe that a person who lacks faith will be burned by the ordeal. The faithful, however, will always be spared injury.

The most remarkable fire walkers in the world are said to be the Sawau tribesmen of the Fiji Islands. They build a circular pit lined with large flat stones, over which they lay a huge log fire. Ten hours later, the

logs are removed. Then a line of Fiji fire walkers, chanting the magical word *"Vitu-O,"* parade across the red-hot stones, their ankles circled by twigs of fresh leaves. Almost without exception the Islanders come through the ordeal without the slightest sign of a burn. And strangely, the leaves also are unharmed.

Students of the practice have also checked carefully to see whether any fire walkers apply some salve or ointment before the ordeal to protect their bodies. None ever do.

Various theories attempt to explain why fire walkers emerge unburned from these tests. Perhaps the fire walker has been entranced or hypnotized to believe he will not be harmed. Or he may be able to control his breathing and pulse in such a way that he becomes oblivious to pain.

Yet none of these theories can explain away the fundamental fact that when flames, coals, or red-hot stones come into contact with human flesh, the flesh normally burns. Thus it is still very much a mystery to science how fire walkers practice their strange ritual unharmed.

The Returning Cats

In the autumn of 1968, a housewife in the suburbs of a large Midwestern city heard scratching sounds at her front door. Puzzled, she went to the door, opened it slowly, and after a few seconds exclaimed, "Jingles!"

Jingles was the family's black-and-white cat. The woman could scarcely believe her eyes because Jingles had been lost for over four weeks—ever since the fam-

ily had missed the cat while on vacation at a lake resort nearly 300 miles away. When, at the end of the vacation, the cat had not shown up, they had had to leave without him.

At first the woman thought she must be mistaken. The cat *looked* like Jingles, but its fur was so matted and dirty that it was hard to tell. Also, one of its ears was torn and there were patches of dried blood on its back. But when the woman saw the grimy white star on the cat's black chest, she knew it must be Jingles.

The woman took Jingles into the bathroom and cleaned him up as best she could. Then she fed him. Except for his torn ear and a slight limp from a cut on one of his legs, Jingles seemed to be in reasonably good shape after his ordeal.

Around the dinner table that night, the family talked about what poor Jingles must have gone through. How had the cat managed to stay alive for all those days and miles? How had it found food? How had the ani-

mal known in which direction the city lay and, once he had reached it, how had he made his way through the busy streets to the correct suburb and his home? The lake resort was so isolated, with twisting, confusing roads leading to it, that Jingles must have had to travel long miles through fields and woods on his way back. There were also several small rivers that the cat must have had to swim across.

As the family shook their heads over these mysteries, Jingles purred happily on the sofa. Already he seemed to have forgotten his terrible experience and was con-

tent simply to be back with the people he loved.

This story is not an unusual one. Cat owners all over the world have reported similar cases of their pets traveling long distances, overcoming tremendous obstacles, to find their way back to their homes. One cat, returning from New Jersey to Brooklyn, must have had to cross the Hudson and East rivers. Whether it used bridges or swam, no one will ever know. Yet it reached home safely. Another cat, lost in the Arizona desert, somehow made its way across the sandy wasteland to its home in Phoenix—over 100 miles away.

Some animal experts have compared this amazing ability of cats to that of homing pigeons. But there is one big difference. Pigeons must be trained by their owners to return. Each training period, they are taken farther and farther from their homes, until they have learned to fly back over great distances. But cats are given no such training. They just seem to *know* the way back.

Does this "homing instinct" have something to do with cats' keen sense of smell? It doesn't seem likely. Even for cats, the smells of home would be too far off for them to sniff their way back. One scientist has suggested that homing pigeons—and perhaps cats as well —somehow use the earth's magnetic field to guide them. But the scientist does not explain how this actually happens. There is also a theory that the cats' strong sense of belonging to certain people and to a certain place somehow furnishes them with a special gift for knowing just how to return to those people and that place. It is still a mystery.

The Snowflake Mystery

The common snowflake is still something of a mystery to scientists. Why does every tiny snow crystal show a hexagonal pattern, with either six sides or six points? When these crystals gather together to form a snow-flake, why does the flake again take on a flat, six-

sided shape instead of some other? And why have no
two snow crystals or snowflakes ever been found to be
exactly alike?

The answers may lie in the way snow is formed in
the atmosphere.

Many people still believe that snow is formed from frozen raindrops. This popular notion should be discarded, along with the belief that lightning will not strike twice in the same place. (It can.) True, raindrops sometimes freeze on the way down from clouds to the earth, but such forms of precipitation are correctly known as sleet or hail. Snow is something else again.

Snow is actually water vapor that has attached itself to very tiny dust particles high in the atmosphere. The water vapor turns directly from its gaseous state into an ice crystal; it does not pass through a liquid stage. These ice crystals can form only when there is sufficient moisture in the air and the dew-point temperature is below freezing.

Once the ice crystals have been formed, they may combine with other crystals and more water vapor to form the larger snow crystals. Eventually they become heavier and fall earthward. Snow crystals are transparent like glass and vary in size from one-fiftieth to one-half of an inch.

In northern countries or high, mountainous regions, snow crystals fall to the ground as individual units. In warmer areas, the snow crystals stick together as they fall. We call these snowflakes, and they can be quite large. Those measuring more than one inch in diameter are not uncommon and are composed of several thousand crystals. But whether snow crystals fall as individual units or gather to form snowflakes, they all are still six-sided or six-pointed—and no two are ever alike.

Many famous people have studied snow. In 157 B.C., a Chinese scholar, Han Ying, observed in one of his poems that most flowers have five petals, but only snow crystals have six. The astronomer Johannes Kepler

(1571–1630) is said to have been the first Westerner to reveal that snow crystals belong to a hexagonal, or six-sided, system in nature. In 1635, the French philosopher René Descartes published sketches of snow crystals, including all the important general types known today.

One of the most ardent students of the structure of snow crystals was Wilson A. Bentley of Jericho, Vermont. Bentley began photographing snow crystals and flakes in 1885 and devoted his whole life to this work. By the time of his death in 1931, he had made over

6,000 photographs of snow. Today Bentley's book *Snow Crystals* is a classic and the pictures in it are world famous for their beauty.

Yet the mysteries concerning snowflakes and crystals still persist. Scientists now know that the hexagonal pattern of snow crystals reflects the same six-sided, latticework arrangement of water molecules in the structure of ice. Nevertheless, in the science of crystallography, there are *seven* different crystal systems: cubic, hexagonal, rhombohedral, tetragonal, orthorhombic, monoclinic, and triclinic. Why do snowflakes and crystals always come in the hexagonal form—in that form alone and no other?

And what of their mysterious and beautiful diversity? Wilson Bentley spent a lifetime examining snowflakes and snow crystals and never found two exactly alike. Nor has anyone else.

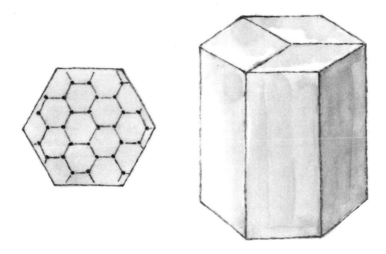

Australian Aborigines Who Use ESP

Before European settlers came to Australia, the continent was inhabited by tall, dark-skinned aborigines. (The word *aborigines* means the earliest inhabitants of a country.) Scientists believe aborigines arrived in Australia about 12,000 years ago from the islands of southeast Asia. When the first Europeans came in 1788, there were probably about 300,000 aborigines living on the continent of Australia.

Today there are about 40,000 full-blooded aborigines and about an equal number of mixed blood. Most of the full-bloods live on reservations—government land set aside for them—in the thinly settled northern areas of the continent. In the more thickly populated parts of Australia, full-blooded aborigines are now very rare.

Many of the aborigines who live on the inland reservations still lead a primitive life much like that of their ancestors. Some are hunters. Some are nomads, or wanderers, who live in tribes and move from place to place in search of food. Like their ancestors, they, too, believe in spells, witch doctors, and other forms of magic.

The aborigines who live outside the reservations have changed their way of life. They no longer live according to strict tribal laws. Some no longer belong to tribes at all. A great number are employed on cattle ranches or farms in the country; others work in the offices and factories of the coastal cities.

But whether aborigines are full-blooded or mixed, whether they cling to the old ways or follow new ones, they often amaze white Australians with an unusual ability. They are able to know things that happen at a distance, often hundreds of miles away. People who have lived among the aborigines or who employ them have reported many striking examples of this strange power.

An aborigine may be away with his employer on a long cattle drive, away from his own people and home for weeks and even months, and he will suddenly announce one day that his father is dead or that there is trouble in the part of the country that he comes from. Later, the employer finds out that the aborigine was quite right.

How can aborigines know such things, when there are no ordinary means of communication whatsoever?

Sometimes the aborigines' knowing-at-a-distance involves a totem. Among primitive peoples, a totem can be an animal or bird or plant that has special meaning for an individual. One story concerns two aborigines who had the same totem.

Billy Combo, a fifty-year-old aborigine, had been in

the hospital but was released after a few days. The doctors said he was well, and to his neighbors and family he appeared to be in good health. A week later, Billy died suddenly of a heart attack.

At the exact time of Billy's death, his nephew, Danny Sambu, who lived sixty miles away, announced that his uncle was dead. Danny Sambu said that he had heard a crow singing and felt beyond any doubt that Billy Combo had died. The crow was the totem of both men.

This strange ability of the aborigines is part of what modern science calls extrasensory perception, or ESP. ESP means gaining knowledge without using the five known senses of seeing, hearing, touching, tasting, and smelling.

Parapsychologists—scientists who study ESP—think

that everybody has this power, but the scientists still don't know how it works. They have also found that in highly developed societies, ESP occurs more rarely than among people like the aborigines, who come from a culture where magic is still practiced and witch doctors are still believed.

One theory says that people in primitive societies regularly relied on ESP to warn them of approaching danger that they could not see, touch, or hear—perhaps a savage animal waiting to attack in the darkness. Over thousands of years, as people became more "civilized," they lost this once razor-sharp faculty. For with civilization came greater safety and better shelter, and people no longer needed ESP as they once did. This theory is just that—a theory. There is still no generally accepted explanation for ESP.

The Self-Destructive Lemmings

Lemmings are small, short-tailed, mouselike animals that live in far northern regions, chiefly in Lapland and the treeless highlands of Norway and Sweden. They have large, hamsterlike heads with small ears and grow to be five or six inches long. Their plump bodies are covered with grayish-brown or golden fur.

For food, lemmings prefer only plant material—roots, stems, leaves, grasses, and seeds. They are very active animals. When they are not gathering food, they dig and run about in long underground runways in the frozen uplands the whole year round.

Lemmings breed and multiply very quickly. Sometimes their numbers become too great for their food supply. This appears to happen every three or four years, especially when the winters have not been too harsh. It is then that their famous migrations, or travels, take place.

Moving from their birthplace in the chilly highlands, great hordes of lemmings gather together—sometimes

38

a million or more—and begin to sweep across the land like a gigantic, living brown blanket.

Because the lemmings live in the mountains, there is only one way for them to go—downhill. Great numbers of them are inescapably funneled down into narrow valleys and cramped gorges. Thus greater numbers of the lemmings are forced uncomfortably together into dense masses of struggling animals. Some are trampled and killed.

As the lemmings descend toward the coast, they ignore all obstacles in their path. Coming to a small river or lake, they swim across. Reaching a cliff, some plunge recklessly over it to their deaths.

Vast numbers of the lemmings are slaughtered along the way by beasts and birds of prey. Foxes, wolves, owls, weasels, hawks, and bears follow the hordes of tiny creatures and feed on them. Many are killed by people because they devour crops and other vegetation. Others fall victim to a disease called lemming fever. Many starve to death. Still others die from no evident cause at all.

Finally, their population greatly diminished, the surviving lemmings reach the coastline—and the sea. There are still many thousands left, but on they go

toward the water. They swarm out onto rocky shoals and tiny beaches. There they immediately plunge into the sea, swim out, and are drowned.

Why do these last survivors apparently take their lives so unhesitatingly? Animal experts aren't sure. Some claim that the lemmings mistake the ocean for just another river and try to cross it. But if that were true, wouldn't at least some see that the ocean is too large and return to shore? Few ever do.

Other experts speak of a mass hysteria, or madness, affecting the little animals due to overcrowding in the

highlands—a death instinct, perhaps, to reduce their numbers so that the few that remain may live on and breed again. For eventually, those pitifully few lemmings remaining in the highlands will rebuild their population. Then another lemming migration will begin.

Whatever the reason for the lemmings' fatal trek, it appears to go against the most basic law of all animal existence—the instinct for self-preservation. Scientists have always thought that animals protect their own lives at any cost. The self-destructive lemmings are still a mystery.

The Water Witches

Searching for hidden things with a divining rod, or a Y-shaped forked stick, is nothing new. People have been doing it for centuries—and they have been *finding* the hidden things, too. In most cases, the divining rod is used to locate water beneath the ground. People who practice this ancient art are known as dowsers, or sometimes as "water witches" because of their uncanny ability to find hidden sources of water.

The ancient Persians, Greeks, and Romans all used the divining rod. Marco Polo, on his famous travels to China, found it in general use throughout the Orient in the late fourteenth and early fifteenth centuries. Georgius Agricola, the Renaissance mining engineer, reported in his books that miners frequently used divining rods to locate veins of iron and other metals. Today, modern "water witches" are still finding water with their forked twigs.

Several kinds of springy wood seem to serve as divining rods. Some dowsers prefer hazel or maple twigs.

Others swear by peach or apple or willow. But the way in which the forked sticks are used is generally the same.

The dowser grasps the forked ends of the twig firmly, with palms upward. As he begins his search for water, the butt of the stick is pointed slightly upward. When he nears water, he can feel the pull as the butt end begins to dip downward. When the dowser is directly over water, the twig points straight down toward the ground.

Perhaps the most famous dowser of modern times was Henry Gross, who, time after time, was able to locate water in many parts of the world. Once Gross actually located water on the parched island of Bermuda without even being there! What Gross did was dowse a large *map* of the island which he had spread out on the floor of his home in *Maine*.

Another case of successful dowsing happened in a small Massachusetts town in 1963. The town officials

had been searching for a lost underground water supply. No one could remember exactly where the water was, and so each summer the town had been forced to ration its scant supply of water. The town's Department of Public Works had tried everything, including a mine detector, to locate the spot where the water was. But nothing had worked.

Then, half jokingly, someone suggested trying a divining rod. The Superintendent of Public Works was skeptical, but finally he thought, why not? Everything else had failed. So some of his men set out with forked twigs in their hands. Presently one of the men, "Dutch" Emery, let out a shout. Emery's stick had moved downward with such force that it had scraped some skin off his thumb. When a five-foot hole was dug at that spot, an old capped pipe leading to the lost water supply was found. When it was uncapped, there proved to be enough pure spring water to serve the town for years.

A scientific explanation for dowsing? There is none as yet. Some researchers into the practice believe that extrasensory perception (ESP) is involved. They suggest that the forked twig held in the hands may somehow serve to tap *knowledge*—in this case, of water—which is beyond the five known human senses. Others think that water may in some way give off faint electromagnetic waves that the dowsers can pick up.

However dowsing works, no fewer than five Nobel Prize winners have endorsed the practice of dowsing as yielding practical results. And a committee of United Nations scientists concluded in 1953: "There can be no doubt that it is a fact." The French Academy of Sciences commented: "It is impossible to deny its existence, although its nature cannot be determined."